PRAYING BY NUMBER

20 Creative Prayer Lessons & Activities

VOLUME TWO

PHYLLIS VOS WEZEMAN

The Pastoral Center

Dedication

To my longtime friend, Mildred Morrison ...

... whose life of dedication to God is an inspiring lesson in prayer! P.V.W.

Acknowledgment

Thanks to Jude Dennis Fournier for collaborating on the lessons and activities in the book, *Praying by Number*.

Jude is Director of Religious Formation at John the XXIII Catholic Community in Albuquerque, New Mexico. His experiences as an educator range from teaching kindergarten in Iowa and high school in Chicago to leading retreats and workshops in countless locations. Jude also serves as a Hospice Chaplain and is involved in mission in places such as El Salvador, Haiti, Kenya, and Malawi. He holds an M.A. in Spirituality.

Jude and Phyllis thrive on finding unique bakeries, coffeeshops, and dessert cafes – purely as settings for planning projects!

ISBN 978-1-949628-05-0
Printed in the United States of America.
10 9 8 7 6 5 4 3 2 1   22 21 20 19 18

Copyright © 1996, 2018 Phyllis Vos Wezeman. All rights reserved. Published by The Pastoral Center / PastoralCenter.com. Permission is given to reproduce the pages in this book as needed for non-commercial use in schools and parish religious education programs. Otherwise, no part of this book may be reproduced in any form or by any means, electronic or mechanical, including photocopying, recording, taping, or via any retrieval system, without the written permission of The Pastoral Center, 1212 Versailles Ave., Alameda, CA 94501. For questions or to order additional copies or licenses, please call 1-844-727-8672 or visit http://pastoral.center.

The Scripture passages contained herein are from the *New Revised Standard Version of the Bible*, copyright © 1989, by the Division of Christian Education of the National Council of Churches in the U.S.A. All rights reserved.

Contents

- (◎) Overview 5
- (21) Meal Time Prayers 7
- (22) Evening Prayer 11
- (23) Psalm 23 15
- (24) 24 Hours 19
- (25) Feast Days 21
- (26) Letters of the Alphabet 25
- (27) Books of the New Testament 27
- (28) Promises of God 31
- (29) Syllables 35
- (30) Pieces of Silver 39
- (31) Prayer Guide 41
- (32) Names of Jesus 43
- (33) Jesus' Passion 45
- (34) Body Postures 47
- (35) Creation 49
- (36) Growth Chart 51
- (37) Symbols 53
- (38) Spontaneous Prayer 63
- (39) Prayer Chain 67
- (40) Wilderness Experiences 71
- (✚) Resources 75
- (✋) About the Author 77

Overview

Prayer is _____. Fill in the blank. This timeless, yet timely, question has been pondered by teachers and students throughout the ages. And, this seemingly simple statement has been completed with answers ranging from a single word to multiple volumes. Webster defines prayer as "the act of praying; an entreaty, supplication; a humble request, as to God; any set formula for this." Commentators and theologians call prayer communicating with God, opening one's life to God, engaging oneself in the purposes of God, and total immersion in the holy presence of God.

Prayer is a vital part of the Christian life. Therefore, it is a subject worth studying. We learn about prayer in many ways. By turning to Scripture, we discover how people in the Old Testament and the New Testament talked with and listened to God. We glean insight into prayer by reading stories of the saints, and we gain instruction about prayer from people of faith today. Perhaps our best guide to learning what prayer is, however, is to actually pray. And, that's what this book provides—twenty prayer opportunities for classes at church and school and for families at home. All lessons are designed to help participants explore and experience various aspects of and approaches to prayer.

This book furnishes twenty lessons based on the topic of prayer. Instruction takes place through participation as students explore and experience inviting, informing, and inspiring activities that are used to impart information and ideas. As a unique feature and a fresh approach, each lesson involves a number, from one to twenty, that becomes the focus for the experience.

Methods used to teach the subject matter incorporate architecture, art, banners/textiles, cartoons, creative writing, dance, drama, games, music, photography, puppetry, and storytelling.

Provided in an easy-to-use format, each lesson is organized into three parts:

- **Goal** states the purpose of the activity,
- **Gather** lists the materials required and suggests steps for advance preparation,
- **Guide** contains complete directions for accomplishing the task.

Prayer is for people of all ages—children, youth, and adults. While these designs are intended for young people in classroom settings, they may be easily adapted for use in small and large group worship, education, outreach, and nurture opportunities. They are ideal for parochial school programs, Sunday school classes, worship centers, children's church, vacation bible school, mid-week ministries, kids' clubs, intergenerational events, before and after school care programs, youth groups, retreats, confirmation classes, family devotions, home schooling, and more.

As you use this resource, may you be as eager and as open as Jesus' disciples were when they pleaded, "Teach us to pray." As teachers and students prepare and participate in activities, may your prayer life be enriched by discovering—or re-discovering—ways to talk with and to listen to God. As you carry the information and insight from the classroom to the world, may the power of prayer be reflected in your daily life.

㉑ Meal Time Prayers

Goal

To use art and creative writing to make table tent prayer kiosks to emphasize the importance of giving thanks before each meal—21 per week.

Gather

- Construction paper, one large sheet for every two students
- Paper, ruled
- Pencils
- Pens
- Resource sheet
  - "21 Questions Game"
- Scissors
- Tape, clear

Advance Preparation

- Duplicate copies of the resource sheet
- Cut 12" x 18" construction paper in half vertically.

Guide

Since this prayer lesson involves the number 21, invite the participants to try to answer 21 questions related to numbers. Distribute a copy of the resource sheet to each participant. As an alternative, verbally ask the questions of the group. Invite the students to guess the number that corresponds with each statement.

Twenty-One Questions

1. Letters of the alphabet [26]
2. Days in a week [7]
3. Digits in a basic zip code [5]
4. Hours in a day [24]
5. Sides on a stop sign [8]
6. Cards in a deck [52]
7. Wonders of the world [7]
8. Days in a week-end [2]
9. Items in a baker's dozen [13]
10. Days in February in a leap year [29]
11. Fruit of the Holy Spirit [9]
12. Minutes in an hour [60]
13. Quarts in a gallon [4]
14. Fingers and toes [20]
15. Days and nights of the great flood [40]
16. Persons in the Trinity [3]
17. Days in a traditional work week [5]
18. Seconds in a minute [60]
19. Inches in a yard [36]
20. Players on a baseball team [9]

▸

For number twenty-one, ask the learners if they can guess what most people do three times a day. Many answers may arise, but "eat" is the correct response for this lesson. Ask the students to name the three meals people eat each day—breakfast, lunch, and dinner. Challenge the group to figure out how many meals most people eat in a week. Of course, the answer is 21: three meals a day times seven days a week equals 21.

Allow time for the learners to share their favorite foods and meals. Explain how important it is to be thankful for God's gift of food. Ask the pupils to name one thing people should do before each meal. The answer is pray. Emphasize the importance of meal time prayers as a way to give praise and thanks to God for all of our gifts.

Tell the group that in this prayer lesson they will be writing meal time prayers and making table-tent kiosks as a way to remember to thank God before breakfast, lunch, and dinner.

Distribute the ruled paper and pencils. Ask the students to write three prayers: one each for breakfast, lunch, and dinner. For example:

Breakfast Prayer

Dear God, thank you for this new day in which to give you praise. Help me to think of you often throughout the day, so that I may be mindful of all that you do for me. Bless the morning and all that it holds and bless this food so that it may give me the nourishment to work hard today. I ask this in Jesus' name. Amen.

Lunch Prayer

Good and loving God, I have completed half of my day and I stop now for a moment to thank and praise you. Be with me as I continue the rest of this day and help me if a problem becomes difficult. My mid-day meal is set before me; I ask your blessing upon it that it will give me the energy I need to finish my day. I ask this in the name of Jesus, who is my friend. Amen.

Dinner Prayer

God, Creator of all that is wonderful, thank you for making me a special part of your creation. Thank you for this day of good work, good play, and good learning. You have given me so many gifts and it makes me happy. Thank you for all the blessings of this day and now bless this meal and all those who made it for me; I realize many people's hands have helped to bring it to this table. Bless it now that it may help prepare me for another day. Amen.

Once the participants have had enough time to write their meal time prayers, encourage the students to read some of them to each other.

Distribute the construction paper, one-half sheet per student. Dispense scissors, pens, and tape. Instruct the learners to fold the paper into three equal sections to form a table tent, also called a kiosk. Tell the students to copy their meal time prayers onto one side of the kiosk, one prayer per section. When the writing is completed, direct the participants to form a triangle and to tape the open-end, or bottom, closed.

Invite the learners to use the prayer kiosk at home. It should be placed in the center of the table for all to see. Pray a prayer before each meal. Encourage the students to think about many people throughout the world who do not have three meals a day and to remember their needs in prayer too.

Dear God, thank you for this new day in which to give you praise. Help me to think of you often throughout the day, so that I may be mindful of all that you do for me. Bless the morning and all that it holds and bless this food so that it may give me the nourishment to work hard today. I ask this in Jesus' name. Amen.

21 Questions Game

1. Letters of the alphabet
2. Days in a week
3. Digits in a basic zip code
4. Hours in a day
5. Sides on a stop sign
6. Cards in a deck
7. Wonders of the world
8. Days in a week-end
9. Items in a baker's dozen
10. Days in February in a leap year
11. Fruit of the Holy Spirit
12. Minutes in an hour
13. Quarts in a gallon
14. Fingers and toes
15. Days and nights of the great flood
16. Persons in the Trinity
17. Days in a traditional work week
18. Seconds in a minute
19. Inches in a yard
20. Players on a baseball team

㉒ Evening Prayer

Goal

To encourage the use of the Bible for evening prayer and to illustrate that Scripture can guide prayer during all times of life.

Gather

- Bibles
- Copy machine
- Markers
- Paper, 8 ½" x 11"
- Paper, glow-in-the-dark (optional)
- Paper, yellow construction
- Pencils
- Resource sheets:
  - "Star Patterns"
  - "Where to Look in the Bible When..."
- Scissors

Advance Preparation

- Duplicate copies of the "Star Patterns" worksheet for the students to share.
- Make a copy of the "Where to Look in the Bible When..." worksheet for each participant.

Guide

Time is every moment there has ever been or ever will be. Time is also a system for measuring duration. Since a day is divided into 24 one-hour segments, many countries of the world, as well as the military, measure time on a 24-hour clock rather than the 12-hour clock that we normally use. A 24-hour system avoids confusion over morning, afternoon, and evening. With a 12-hour system, if someone says it's 10:00 o'clock, that could mean its two hours before noon or two hours before midnight. Using a 24-hour clock, 10:00 hours is morning and 22:00 hours is night.

The Bible is a book that meets our needs at any time of the day. The Bible is also our guide for prayer, the way we communicate with God, through all the times of our lives. Many people turn to the words of the Bible to help them put their thoughts and feelings into prayers. Scripture verses can help us pray when we are happy or sad, calm or afraid, well or sick. Many Bibles and devotional guides contain a list of "Where to Look When...." In this lesson, this type of list will be used as a guide for evening prayer.

Hand out the "Where to Look in the Bible When..." resource sheet to each participant.

Distribute the Bibles and invite the participants to choose two or three themes from the list that are of interest to them and to look up the passages. Provide time for locating and reading the verses.

Encourage the learners to share what was gleaned from the Bible. What did the passage say? Did it offer advice? Did it provide an answer? Invite participants to read selections aloud for further discussion.

▸

Once everyone has had an opportunity to share, explain that these passages are a good guide to use when we want to express our emotions in the form of prayers. Each person will have the opportunity to make 22 stars and to print Scripture references on them that can be used as an aid to evening prayer. The "Where to Look in the Bible When..." stars may be taken home and, with permission, attached to the walls or ceiling of the bedroom.

Distribute glow-in-the-dark sheets or yellow construction paper along with star patterns, scissors, pencils, and markers. The glow-in-the-dark paper will add to the night time, evening prayer atmosphere. Instruct the students to trace and cut 22 stars from the paper. Once the stars are prepared, direct the group to letter a different "Where to Look..." word and Scripture reference on each shape. For example:

- Afraid: Psalm 27
- Guilty: Psalm 51
- Hurting: Hebrews 12
- Tempted: James 1

Note that the word and the reference should be written on the same side of the star. Encourage participants to use the markers to decorate or illustrate each star.

Invite the pupils to take the stars home and to ask permission to tape them to a bedroom wall or ceiling. Encourage them to use the stars as a guide for prayer before bed time—at 22:00 hours (10:00 p.m.) or another time. The stars should serve as a reminder that God is present and available to us through prayer—all the time!

Star Patterns

Where to Look in the Bible When...

God seems far away: Psalm 139

People fail you: Psalm 27

You feel defeated: Acts 1-8

You feel guilty: Psalm 51; 1 John 1-2

You feel happy: Psalm 95

You feel lonely: Luke 6

You feel sorrowful: Psalm 46

You have sinned: Psalm 51

You leave home to travel: Psalm 121

You need assurance: Romans 8

You need rest and peace: Matthew 12:25-30

You need to know God's will for your life: Proverbs 3:1-6

You need to make a decision: Proverbs 3

You want courage: Joshua 1:1-9

You wonder about death: 1 Corinthians 15

You're afraid: Psalms 27, 91, 139

You're discouraged: Psalm 34

You're hurting: Hebrews 12

You're sick: Psalm 41

You're tempted: James 1; 1 Corinthians 10

You're tired: Psalm 23

You're trying to figure out right and wrong: Colossians 2

PRAYING BY NUMBER

23 Psalm 23

Goal

To use Psalm 23 in a prayer service.

Gather

- Bible
- Candle, white
- Cloth to cover prayer table
- Copy machine
- Equipment to play recorded music
- Matches
- Paper, white construction
- Pencils
- Recording of tranquil music
- Resource sheets:
  - "Sheep Patterns"
  - "Psalm 23 Responsive Reading"
- Scissors
- Table

Advance Preparation

- Make copies of the "Sheep Patterns" resource sheet. Cut sheep out of white construction paper, one per participant.
- Duplicate the "Psalm 23 Responsive Reading" resource sheet.
- Set a table in a prominent place in the gathering space.

Guide

For many people, Psalm 23 is their favorite passage of Scripture. In this familiar chapter, God is seen as a caring shepherd and a dependable guide. We, like sheep, must follow God and obey God's commands. God is our only hope for eternal life and security. In this lesson Psalm 23 is used as the basis of a prayer service. Participants will have the opportunity to read the Psalm and to write phrases of a litany—a prayer in which people speak responsively—to illustrate additional metaphors describing God.

Invite the group to sit around the table that has been positioned in a prominent location in the gathering space. Place the prayer cloth, candle, and Bible on the table. Distribute copies of Psalm 23 and tell the students that it will be read responsively during the prayer service. Organize the participants into two groups. Open the Bible to Psalm 23, light the candle, and begin playing tranquil background music. Encourage silence as worship begins.

Psalm 23 Prayer Service

Opening prayer

Lord, Jesus, Shepherd of us all, you call us together and invite us to be the sheep of your flock. We know that if we stray from your care, you will find us and lead us back. We gather now to give you thanks and praise as our Shepherd who goes in search of the lost sheep. Amen.

Psalm 23

Read responsively using the resource sheet.

▸

Prayer Response: A Litany

Explain that in Psalm 23 God is described as a shepherd. Throughout the Bible and in our everyday lives, God is experienced in many ways—for example, as a friend, a guide, or a healer.

Distribute a construction paper sheep and a pencil to each participant. Instruct the worshipers to complete the statement: The Lord is my _____. Tell the group that the symbols will be used in a litany—a responsive prayer—based on Psalm 23. Invite each student to write a word on the paper sheep. Allow time for ideas as well as for reflection.

Once everyone has completed the task, begin the litany by inviting the learners to take turns reading their metaphors. After each phrase is read, the sheep should be placed on the prayer table. Use the following format for the litany:

Reader: The Lord is my _____.

All: We praise your holy name.

Sample Litany

Reader: The Lord is my advocate.
   All: We praise your holy name.

Reader: The Lord is my comfort.
   All: We praise your holy name.

Reader: The Lord is my companion.
   All: We praise your holy name.

Reader: The Lord is my consoler.
   All: We praise your holy name.

Reader: The Lord is my counselor.
   All: We praise your holy name.

Reader: The Lord is my defense.
   All: We praise your holy name.

Reader: The Lord is my friend.
   All: We praise your holy name.

Reader: The Lord is my God.
   All: We praise your holy name.

Reader: The Lord is my guide.
   All: We praise your holy name.

Reader: The Lord is my healer.
   All: We praise your holy name.

Reader: The Lord is my hope.
   All: We praise your holy name.

Reader: The Lord is my light.
   All: We praise your holy name.

Reader: The Lord is my life.
   All: We praise your holy name.

Reader: The Lord is my love.
   All: We praise your holy name.

Reader: The Lord is my mentor.
   All: We praise your holy name.

Reader: The Lord is my Messiah.
   All: We praise your holy name.

Reader: The Lord is my redemption.
   All: We praise your holy name.

Reader: The Lord is my salvation.
   All: We praise your holy name.

Reader: The Lord is my savior.
   All: We praise your holy name.

Reader: The Lord is my spirit.
   All: We praise your holy name.

Reader: The Lord is my teacher.
   All: We praise your holy name.

Reader: The Lord is my truth.
   All: We praise your holy name.

Reader: The Lord is my way.
   All: We praise your holy name.

At the end of the litany, stand and form a circle around the prayer table. Silently reflect on the responses to the statement "The Lord is my _____."

Closing Prayer

Lord, God of all. You are many things to many people. Help us to remember your constant love. We know that we make mistakes and often make the wrong choices; but you always love us as your children, no matter what we do. Help us to spend our lives praising your holy name. Amen.

Sheep Patterns

Psalm 23 Responsive Reading

Right

The Lord is my shepherd,
*   I shall not want.*
He makes me lie down in green pastures;
*   he leads me beside still waters;*
*   he restores my soul.*

Left

He leads me in right paths
*   for his name's sake.*
Even though I walk through the darkest valley,
*   I fear no evil;*
for you are with me;
*   your rod and your staff—*
*   they comfort me.*

Right

You prepare a table before me
*   in the presence of my enemies;*
you anoint my head with oil;
*   my cup overflows.*

Left

Surely goodness and mercy shall follow me
*   all the days of my life,*
and I shall dwell in the house of the Lord
*   my whole life long.*

㉔ 24 Hours

Goal

To organize and participate in a twenty-four-hour prayer vigil.

Gather

> Markers
> Poster board
> Supplies, varied with selected activities

Guide

Twenty-four _____. Fill in the blank. The usual response is hours. Twenty-four hours _____. The response might be "in a day." In this lesson, the response to the words 24 hours is prayer vigil!

A prayer vigil is a time set aside for continuous prayer. Generally, the prayer is focused on one or more specific topics. Themes could center on a particular need in the congregation; a special day such as National Day of Prayer; a season like Advent; or a response to a local, regional, national, or international situation. Explain the concept of a prayer vigil to the students and invite them to organize and participate in one.

Begin by answering the following questions.

1. What is the purpose of the prayer vigil?

Will the vigil be held to offer physical, emotional, and spiritual support to someone who is sick? Will the vigil emphasize a special day or season, such as a Holy Week theme? Will the prayer time be in response to an ongoing need such as world peace or to an immediate crisis like a natural disaster? Clearly establish the purpose of the vigil before proceeding!

▸

2. Who will participate in the prayer vigil?

Will it just be the class or possibly the class and their families? Will other classes or the whole parish be invited to take part in the event?

3. How long will the prayer vigil be?

Twenty-four hours is a good goal but be realistic! Since people must pray continuously during the designated amount of time, this could be an impossible aim to accomplish. Factors determining the answer to this question include the number of participants and their ages. If just one class will be involved, choose a short, manageable amount of time. If the entire parish will participate, a longer amount of time is possible.

4. How long will each person pray?

This question is answered by the length of the vigil and the number of people involved. If the entire congregation is invited to pray for 24 hours, 15-minute intervals per person would work. If fewer people are involved, longer amounts of time are needed.

5. When will the prayer vigil be held?

Determine the date. If school age children are involved, the event should probably take place on a weekend rather than a weeknight. If only one class is responsible, the prayer vigil could be scheduled during their normal meeting time.

6. Where will the prayer vigil take place?

It could be in the sanctuary, chapel, classroom, or in homes. Homes might be preferred if people sign up to pray during the night.

7. How will the prayer vigil be advertised?

If more than the class participates, make arrangements to place announcements in parish bulletins or other publications.

8. Who will pray when?

Prepare a poster that provides information on the purpose of the prayer vigil, as well as the date, time, and location. Draw lines for time slots marked in equal increments so participants can sign up to pray at specific times. Place the poster on an easel or bulletin board and set it in a place where many people will see it. Attach a pen or pencil to the display.

9. What will be needed at the actual prayer vigil?

Arrange help as anticipated, for example, a custodian to open the building if the event is held at church; adult volunteers to supervise the vigil; and volunteers to call to remind participants of their pledged time.

10. How will people know what to do?

Prepare a one-page prayer guide. It should include purpose, date, place, and assigned prayer time. Include suggested prayer topics, list Scripture passages for meditation, and offer information that might be helpful.

Hold the actual prayer vigil. Before, during, and after the prayer vigil experience, remind the class of the familiar words of Matthew 7:7-8: "Ask, and it will be given you; search, and you will find; knock, and the door will be opened for you. For everyone who asks receives, and everyone who searches finds, and for everyone who knocks, the door will be opened." God is eager to hear—and answer—our prayers 24 hours a day!

25 Feast Days

Goal

To interpret the mysteries of the faith through art while praying the decades of the rosary.

Gather

- Art to illustrate the 15 decades of the rosary
- Computer, projector, and screen (optional)
- Bibles
- Resource sheet:
  - "Sources of Art to Illustrate the Rosary"
- Rosaries, one per person

Advance Preparation

Using the suggestions on the resource sheet, find examples to illustrate each Mystery.

Guide

Two of the feast days observed by the church have the number 25 in common: both emphasize the life of Mary. The Feast of the Annunciation, the angel's announcement that Mary would be the mother of God's son, Jesus, is commemorated March 25, and Christmas, the day Mary gave birth to the savior of the world, is celebrated on December 25. One way the church has honored Mary through the ages is by praying the rosary. To pray the rosary is to contemplate, alongside Mary, the Lord made flesh, crucified, and raised for our salvation.

The complete rosary is a prayer comprising 150 "Hail Marys" divided into 15 decades, each of which serve as a meditation on a different mystery of Christ. The name "rosary" is also given to the beads themselves, which are separated into groups of ten by larger individual beads.

In this prayer lesson, participants will view classical and contemporary art while they pray the rosary. Through this experience of meditating on the joyful, sorrowful, and glorious mysteries of Christ, emphasis will be placed on comprehending the words that are spoken, rather than repeating them routinely. As students see and say this classic prayer, it will hopefully help them understand what they believe.

Pope Paul VI spoke of the rosary as a "compendium of the entire Gospel" and Cardinal Newman stated, "It enables us, so to speak, to hold our entire faith in the hand." The joyful, sorrowful, and glorious mysteries correspond to the fundamental aspects of the mystery of Christ: the Incarnation, Passion, and Resurrection. Review the 15 mysteries with the class and look up the Scripture passages. Encourage volunteers to share and to read this information.

▸

The mysteries are:

The Five Joyful Mysteries

1. *Annunciation (Luke 1:26-38)*
2. *Visitation (Luke 1:39-45)*
3. *Nativity (Luke 2:1-20)*
4. *Presentation (Luke 2:22-38)*
5. *Finding in the Temple (Luke 2:41-51)*

The Five Sorrowful Mysteries

6. *Agony in the garden (Matthew 26:26-43)*
7. *Scourging (Luke 22:63-65)*
8. *Crowning with thorns (Mark 15:16-20)*
9. *Carrying of the cross (Luke 23:26-28)*
10. *Crucifixion (Mark 15:33-39)*

The Five Glorious Mysteries

11. *Resurrection (Mark 16:1-7)*
12. *Ascension (Acts 1:6-11)*
13. *Descent of the Holy Spirit (Acts 1:6-11)*
14. *Assumption (Tradition)*
15. *Coronation (Tradition)*

Tell the class that artists throughout history have illustrated these Scripture stories through a variety of methods and materials. One way is through classical and contemporary paintings. As a way of meditating on each mystery while praying the rosary, use visuals to enrich the experience. "Good art nurtures the inner eye, the eye of the soul, and when the inner eye is nurtured, holiness grows." (Manternach, Janaan with Carl J. Pfeifer. *And the Children Pray.* Notre Dame, IN: Ave Maria Press, 1983, p.140) As an image depicting each mystery is displayed, students will have the opportunity to meditate on the Scripture story while repeating the prayers associated with the decade.

Prepare the class for a time of contemplative prayer. Indicate whether the prayers will be offered aloud as a group or silently by each person. Distribute a rosary to each pupil or ask the students to take out their own. Display the first picture on a table or a screen. Begin the first decade by praying the "Our Father," continue by repeating fifteen "Hail Marys," and conclude by saying the "Gloria." Display the second picture and repeat the process until the 15 decades are completed. Conclude with a time of silent reflection.

Sources of Art to Illustrate the Rosary

For three of the decades in the joyful mysteries, here is an example of art to use:

The Annunciation

- "The Annunciation" by Correggio
- "The Annunciation" by Leonardo Da Vinci
- "The Annunciation" by Fra Filippo Lippi

The Nativity

- "The Virgin Adoring the Child" by Botticelli
- "Nativity" by El Greco
- "Holy Family" by Michelangelo

The Presentation

- "The Presentation" by Hans Memling

Use the list of suggested places and ways to discover art to use with this lesson. Ideas include:

- Complete pictures in specialized coloring books like:
  - Sibbett, Ed, Jr. *Cathedral Stained Glass Coloring Book.* New York: Dover Publications, 1980.
- Discover drawings in prayer books.
- Examine pictures in Bibles.
- Find information in encyclopedias.
- Locate illustrations in Bible story books.
- Look in art books which contain reproductions of paintings. Sources include:
  - Taylor, Francis Henry. *Fifty Centuries of Art.* New York: Harper and Brothers, 1954.
  - Walker, John. *National Gallery of Art, Washington.* New York: Harry N. Abrams, 1975.
- Notice the art on:
  - Christmas and Easter cards
  - Commemorative plates
  - Note cards and stationery
  - Postage stamps
  - Postcards
  - Posters
  - Prayer cards.
- Page through books on periods of art such as Middle Ages, Renaissance, Spanish, and French.
- Read biographies of artists.
- Research other types of art besides painting:
  - Altar pieces
  - Medallions
  - Mosaics
  - Sculpture
  - Stained glass
  - Tapestries
  - Vestments
- Search the internet for art related to the topics of each mystery.
- Tour a church and discover its art.
- View photo sets, such as:
  - Sound/Sight Library. *The Christmas Story.* New York: The Metropolitan Museum of Art, n.d.
- Visit an art museum and view the collection of paintings and other art. As an optional activity, arrangements might be made to hold the prayer experience in this location.
- Watch a film or video about paintings and painters

26 Letters of the Alphabet

Goal

To create A-Z prayers and ribbon banners as a way to thank God for blessings.

Gather

- Crayons or markers
- Glue
- Paper, construction
- Ribbon
- Scissors
- Tape, masking or push pins

Guide

Apples. Babies. Cats. Dogs. There are so many things for which to be thankful! God provides for people's physical, emotional, and spiritual needs in numerous ways. In fact, everyone could go through the 26 letters of the alphabet—many times—naming God's blessings. Try it! Besides verbalizing the suggestions, record them in a visual way by making ribbon banners.

Gather the group in a circle on the floor, on chairs, or around tables. Tell the participants that they will each name an item for which they are thankful. The first person will identify something that begins with the letter A, and the rest of the players will progress through the entire alphabet, from B-Z, adding ideas. Each person takes a turn saying: "I am thankful for _____." The first person fills in the blank with an item beginning with the letter A, such as apples. Each successive person repeats the sentence as the previous one said it, and then adds the phrase "and _____," filling in the blank with an item beginning with the next letter of the alphabet. For example, the second person might say "I am thankful for apples and books." If a person has difficulty remembering what was previously said, encourage the rest of the group to give hints and help. Continue through the entire alphabet until something is named for each letter.

Structure the activity by suggesting that the players name items or ideas for various categories, such as animals, Bible stories, flowers, hobbies, ice cream flavors, people, places, or professions. The list is endless! Continue the process until the participants tire of the activity or run out of suggestions.

▸

Use the ideas that were verbalized and make visual reminders of A-Z thankfulness. To form individual ribbon banners, provide each person with a long strip of one-inch wide ribbon. Offer construction paper, scissors, markers, and glue. Tell each person to draw, cut, or trace a symbol of thanks for each letter of the alphabet. In order, from A-Z, attach the pieces vertically to the strip of ribbon. For a group project, invite each person to choose a different letter of the alphabet, until all twenty-six are selected, and to create designs depicting thankfulness. Specify that each illustration should be of an item or idea beginning with the assigned letter.

When the individual or group banners are completed, tape or tack the top of each strip to a wall or bulletin board to display the finished projects. Conclude by offering a prayer thanking God for every blessing, named and unnamed, from A-Z.

27 Books of the New Testament

Goal

To create praying hands shape books containing a guideline for prayer from each book of the New Testament.

Gather

- Bibles
- Hole punch
- Markers
- Newsprint
- Paper, construction
- Pencils
- Resource sheet:
  - "New Testament Prayer Guide"
- Scissors
- Twine or yarn

Advance Preparation

- Duplicate resource sheet.

Guide

In this lesson participants will search the 27 books of the New Testament to discover the Bible's guidelines on prayer. Lesson 27 can be used as one or several sessions. Explain the project and construct the shape books during one class and look up the passages in other meetings. As a journaling project, read and reflect on a different passage each day. Collect the shape books each time they are used.

To begin, hold up a Bible and ask volunteers to answer these questions:

- What is the name of this book? [The Bible]
- How many parts are in the Bible? [Two]
- What are the two parts? [The Old Testament (Hebrew Bible) and the New Testament]
- How many books are contained in the New Testament? [27]

Challenge the group to name the 27 books of the New Testament. Write the responses on newsprint. The books are:

- Matthew
- Mark
- Luke
- John
- Acts
- Romans
- 1 Corinthians
- 2 Corinthians
- Galatians
- Ephesians
- Philippians
- Colossians
- 1 Thessalonians
- 2 Thessalonians
- 1 Timothy
- 2 Timothy
- Titus
- Philemon
- Hebrews
- James
- 1 Peter
- 2 Peter
- 1 John
- 2 John
- 3 John
- Jude
- Revelation

▶

If the participants have difficulty naming the books, distribute Bibles and direct the group to the table of contents or tell them to page through the New Testament to find the names. Review the names of the books in order.

Continue by asking the group a few more questions, for example:

- Do you pray? [Ask for a show of hands.]
- When do you pray? [Before meals; at bedtime]
- How do you pray? [Eyes closed; hands folded]
- What do you say? [Responses may vary]
- What does the Bible teach us about prayer? [A lot!]

Remind the group that every book of the New Testament offers guidelines for prayer. In this lesson, participants will have the opportunity to search the Scriptures to see what they have to say about prayer and to make a praying hands shape book to record the lessons they learn.

Distribute construction paper, pencils, and scissors. Tell the learners to trace one hand onto construction paper—palms down, fingers together, thumb out—and to cut out the shape. It may be easier to have partners take turns tracing each other's hands.

Using the hand as a pattern, participants should trace and cut 15 more hands from construction paper. Tell the students to stack the pages neatly so they all line up. Once the books are assembled, punch two holes at the base of the wrist and tie the sheets together with twine or yarn. The shape book should look like hands that open and close in prayer. Instruct the learners to print the words "New Testament Prayer Guide" on the front cover of the book and to write their name and age on the second sheet. In addition to the back cover, there are now 27 front and back sides—one page for a prayer-related Scripture reference from each book of the New Testament.

Students may work alone or in small groups to complete the Scripture search activity. Distribute a Bible and a resource sheet to each person or team. Tell the listeners to look up a Bible verse in each New Testament book and discover what it teaches about prayer. Instruct the learners to write the name of the book and its reference on the top of the page and to record a few words about its teaching on prayer in the remaining space. For example, Matthew 6:5-8 tells us to pray to God in private, not to show off to others. God knows what is in our heart.

Once the entire lesson is completed, invite the participants to take the shape books home to use as a prayer guide during family or personal devotions.

New Testament Prayer Guide

1. Matthew 6:5-8
2. Mark 7:6-7
3. Luke 11:2-13
4. John 14:13-14
5. Acts 4:24-30
6. Romans 8:26
7. 1 Corinthians 14:15
8. 2 Corinthians 6:16-18
9. Galatians 2:19-20
10. Ephesians 6:18
11. Philippians 4:6-7
12. Colossians 4:2
13. 1 Thessalonians 5:17
14. 2 Thessalonians 1:11
15. 1 Timothy 2:1-3
16. 2 Timothy 2:11-13
17. Titus 2:11-14
18. Philemon 17-20
19. Hebrews 5:7-9
20. James 5:16-18
21. 1 Peter 2:4-5
22. 2 Peter 1:19
23. 1 John 5:14-15
24. 2 John 3
25. 3 John 11
26. Jude 24-25
27. Revelation 4:8-11, 5:9-14

PRAYING BY NUMBER

28 Promises of God

Goal

To weave a rainbow symbolizing the promises of God.

Gather

- Basket or box
- Bible
- Cardboard, 3' x 5', or large wooden frame
- Copy machine
- Dictionary
- Knife, utility type
- Markers, permanent
- Materials for weaving (rainbow colors): bags, plastic; fabric; paper; ribbon, wide; and yarn, heavy
- Paper
- String, heavy
- Resource sheets:
    - "Scripture Promises"
    - "Frame for Weaving"
- Scissors
- Slats, wooden

Advance Preparation

- Prepare the cardboard frame for the weaving by cutting one-inch slits into the top and bottom of the piece, approximately one inch apart. Wrap the cardboard by running a continuous piece of heavy string or twine from one side to the other, through each slit.
- Cut the weaving materials into strips (one-inch wide and four to five feet long). Four strips of each color of the rainbow—red, orange, yellow, green, blue, indigo, and violet—are needed for this project. Place the pieces in a basket or box.
- Duplicate resource sheet.

Guide

I promise! Promises are easy to make; sometimes they are hard to keep—for us, at least. The Bible, however, is filled with promises from God: promises that God made; promises that God kept; promises that God will keep.

One of the most familiar promises in the Bible is found in the story of Noah and the Ark. In Genesis 9:8-17, God's promise is confirmed by a special symbol: the rainbow. Look up the passage and read it aloud. In this prayer lesson, participants have the opportunity to look up twenty-eight promises of God and to create a "rainbow" weaving to use on a prayer table or in a worship center.

Look up the word "promise" in a dictionary. Simply stated, a promise is an agreement to do or not to do something. Tell the group that God's Word, the Bible, is filled with promises. They will work together to discover 28 of them. Organize the class into seven pairs or small groups. Distribute the resource sheet.

Assign each group four Scripture passages to look up and read. Direct them to mark each location with a scrap of paper for future reference.

Show the learners the weaving background and explain that weaving is an art form which combines a variety of strands or pieces into a beautiful blend of texture, fabric, and design. Individually and collectively, they will be creating a rainbow weaving to help them visualize the promises of God. It will be placed on a prayer table or displayed in a worship center. Since there are seven colors in a rainbow, and the number emphasized in this prayer lesson is 28, each group will prepare four promise strips to add to the frame.

▶

Distribute four strips of material, each representing a different color of the rainbow, and permanent markers to each group. Direct the teams to write one of their assigned promises on each piece. The Scripture reference—book, chapter, and verse—may be printed, the verse(s) could be lettered, or a summary of the promise might be written. Allow time for the groups to prepare the promise strips.

When the weaving materials are completed, gather the group in a circle on the floor or on chairs. Place the cardboard frame in the center of the space. Take turns having each group come forward and weave their four strips into the background piece. Promise passages may be read or summarized as the weaving takes place. After completing each color, invite the class to repeat the prayer: "Thank you, God, for keeping your promises." Continue the process until all seven colors have been woven into the frame. Periodically push the materials closer together to allow room for new pieces. To make the piece more secure, place a wooden slat into the weaving after several colors have been inserted.

Conclude the prayer lesson by re-reading God's promise to Noah and by repeating the phrase "Thank you, God, for keeping your promises." Remind the group that God's greatest promise—to send us a Savior—was fulfilled in the person and work of Jesus.

Scripture Promises

Genesis 8:21	John 14:12
Joshua 1:9	John 14:27
Isaiah 43:1-2	John 15:7
Isaiah 44:1-2	Acts 2:8
Jeremiah 1:7-8	Acts 2:38-39
Jeremiah 29:11-13	Romans 3:23-24
Matthew 6:31-33	Romans 8:38-39
Matthew 7:7-8	1 Corinthians 10:13
Matthew 11:28-30	1 Corinthians 15:22
Matthew 28:20b	2 Corinthians 6:16b-7:1a
Mark 10:14	Galatians 5:22-23b
John 11:25-26	Philippians 4:1a
John 14:3	Revelation 3:20
John 14:6	Revelation 21:3-4

29 Syllables

Goal

To write twenty-nine syllable poems to be used as prayers.

Gather

- Candle
- Chalkboard and chalk, computer and screen, or newsprint and marker
- Equipment to play recorded music
- Paper, ruled
- Matches
- Pencils
- Pens
- Poetry patterns such as cinquain, haiku, and tanka
- Recording of tranquil music
- Resource sheet:
  - "Poetry Patterns"

Advance Preparation

Prepare poetry patterns and examples on a chalkboard, computer, or newsprint.

Guide

Poetry may be defined as an arrangement of words in a style that is more imaginative than ordinary speech. Some poems are written according to a pattern of rhyme and rhythm; others are free from structure. Regardless of the format, poems are used to express thoughts and feelings. In this lesson, 29 syllable poems will be written and used as prayers.

Begin by asking someone to define the word poetry. Ask the group to name as many different types of poems as possible. The list may include acrostic, ballad, cinquain, couplet, diamond, epic, free verse, haiku, limerick, ode, sonnet, and tanka. Most of these types of poems have something in common: they are written according to a formula or pattern.

A poetry pattern is a specific arrangement of syllables, words, or lines. Explain that a syllable is a word or part of a word pronounced with a single, uninterrupted sounding of the voice. Tell the students that they will have the opportunity to experiment with a variety of formulas to write poems. First, they will write on a topic of their choice, or the assigned subject, and then they will write poems to be used as prayers. Provide examples of poetry patterns, such as the top three found on the resource sheet.

Invite the participants to select one of these patterns and to write a poem. Assign a subject such as family, food, friends, nature, school, sports, or vacation or tell the students to pick a topic of interest to them. Distribute paper and pens or pencils and guide the writing process. Once the poetry has been completed ask for volunteers to share the results.

▸

Challenge the learners to design a new poetry pattern containing 29 syllables and to create poems that can be offered as prayers. Topics could focus on God, Jesus, life, love, thankfulness, and so forth. Explain that the words and lines of the poems can be arranged in any way, but no more or less than 29 syllables can be used.

Share examples of 29 syllable poetry formulas, as found at the bottom of the resource sheet.

Invite the learners to have fun experimenting with this new pattern for writing poetry. Challenge each pupil to write two or three prayer poems. Distribute additional paper, if needed. Once all participants have written several poems, conclude the lesson with a prayer service.

Ask the group to form a circle, by sitting on the floor or on chairs or by standing together. Place a candle in the center of the circle for all to see. Ignite the candle and ask those gathered to be silent. Play soft background music for added reflection while prayer poems are read aloud. Encourage each participant to share one poem as prayer, moving around the circle to be sure everyone has a turn. End with a moment of silent reflection.

Poetry Patterns

Cinquain

Poem containing five lines

Line 1 - A one-word noun

Line 2 - Two adjectives that describe the noun

Line 3 - Three "ing" words that describe the noun

Line 4 - Four words that express a feeling about the noun

Line 5 - One word that is a synonym for the noun

Example:
John
Painter, Repairer
Sharing, Caring, Giving
Helping those in need
Peacemaker

Haiku

Poetry containing three lines

Line 1 - 5 syllables

Line 2 - 7 syllables

Line 3 - 5 syllables

Example:
Tall, thrashing corn stalks
golden in the wind and sun
remind me of home

Tanka

Poetry containing five lines

Line 1 - 5 syllables

Line 2 - 7 syllables

Line 3 - 5 syllables

Line 4 - 7 syllables

Line 5 - 7 syllables

Example:
Great mighty mountain
You beckon to us, come, see
We sought your beauty
along the creeks and rivers
in the warm light of the day

Twenty-Nine Syllable Poem

Poem containing four lines

Line 1 - 2 syllables

Line 2 - 9 syllables

Line 3 - 9 syllables

Line 4 - 9 syllables

Example:
Wind, fire,
Spirit, breath of God, breathing newness
in all of creation your breath is
upon us. Change our lives for You, God.

Poem containing five lines

Line 1 - 5 syllables

Line 2 - 7 syllables

Line 3 - 5 syllables

Line 4 - 7 syllables

Line 5 - 5 syllables

Example:
Messiah, our God,
Immanuel, God with us.
Come, in winter cold
a star shines in the night sky,
light our way, Child.

Poem containing six lines

Line 1 - 1 syllable

Line 2 - 4 syllables

Line 3 - 6 syllables

Line 4 - 8 syllables

Line 5 - 4 syllables

Line 6 - 6 syllables

Example:
Christ,
Incarnation,
born of the Virgin Mary
to journey among God's people
in time and place,
in Word and bread.

30 Pieces of Silver

Goal

To help learners understand the depth of God's forgiveness during times of personal betrayal.

Gather

- Basket
- Bible
- Can, large
- Candle
- Cloth for prayer table
- Coins, 30 silver such as nickels, dimes, quarters
- Equipment to play recording
- Matches
- Money, paper play type
- Music or recording for "Lord Teach Us to Pray" by Joe Wise
- Pencils
- Pouch, cloth or leather
- Table

Advance Preparation

- Find or make play money and place it in a basket.
- Put thirty silver coins in the pouch.
- Arrange for adult supervision during the symbolic burning portion of the prayer service.

Guide

How many coins did Judas receive when he arranged to lead Jesus into the hands of his enemies? Judas collected thirty pieces of silver, about the price of a slave in those days, for this act of betrayal. Scripture records the story in:

- Matthew 26:14, 20-25, 47-56; 27:3-10
- Mark 14:10-11, 17-21, 43-50
- Luke 22:3-6, 14-23, 47-53
- John 13:21-30; 18:1-11

After Judas realized the severity of the situation, he tried to return the money to the high priest, who would not take it back. Overcome with guilt, Judas threw the thirty pieces of silver on the floor, saying, "I have sinned in that I have betrayed innocent blood."

Jesus died on the cross to offer forgiveness to all who believe in him. Instead of being overcome with guilt, Judas could have experienced God's abundant love—if he had only repented and asked for forgiveness. Judas, however, is not the only one who fails to ask for forgiveness. We all do! Use the prayer service in this lesson as an opportunity to remind the participants of the depth of God's forgiveness during times of personal betrayal.

Before beginning the prayer service, summarize the story of Jesus' betrayal. Be sure that the students understand the meaning of the word betrayal: to deceive. Also, be sure that the group realizes that examples of betrayal occur every day. Telling a secret betrays a confidence; throwing a game betrays a team.

Prepare the table for the prayer service. Cover the table with the cloth and place the candle, matches, Bible, pouch containing thirty silver coins, basket with paper money, large empty coffee can, and pencils on it. Gather the group in the worship space and encourage silence as the prayer begins.

Thirty Pieces of Silver Prayer Service

Opening Song

"Lord Teach Us to Pray" by Joe Wise

Opening Prayer

Leader: All merciful and loving God, we Your children come to You for forgiveness. We too, like Judas, betray Your love and kindness by not being true to the person of Your son and our brother, Jesus. Jesus is the true Redeemer of all sin. Help us to remember that our actions and words can bring about healing or they can bring about hurt. Guide us in our every move, so that all our living is done to bring about a Kingdom of love and not of betrayal.

All: We say Amen, because we believe.

First Reader: Matthew 26:14-16

Then one of the twelve, who was called Judas Iscariot, went to the chief priests and said, "What will you give me if I betray him to you?" They paid him thirty pieces of silver. And from that moment he began to look for an opportunity to betray him.

At the end of this reading open pouch and spill thirty coins onto the prayer table.

Pause for silence.

Second Reader: Matthew 26:20-25

When it was evening, he took his place with the twelve; and while they were eating, he said, "Truly I tell you, one of you will betray me." And they became greatly distressed and began to say to him one after another, "Surely not I, Lord?" He answered, "The one who has dipped his hand into the bowl with me will betray me. The Son of Man goes as it is written of him, but woe to that one by whom the Son of Man is betrayed! It would have been better for that one not to have been born." Judas, who betrayed him, said, "Surely not I, Rabbi?" He replied, "You have said so."

Pause for silence.

Third Reader: Matthew 26:47-50

While he was still speaking, Judas, one of the twelve, arrived; with him was a large crowd with swords and clubs, from the chief priests and the elders of the people. Now the betrayer had given them a sign, saying, "The one I will kiss is the man; arrest him." At once he came up to Jesus and said, "Greetings, Rabbi!" and kissed him. Jesus said to him, "Friend, do what you are here to do." Then they came and laid hands on Jesus and arrested him.

Pause for silence

Prayer Response

Pass the basket holding the paper play money. Invite each participant to take one bill. Instruct the learners to reflect on a way they have betrayed Jesus and his love for them. Maybe it was a time where they were unkind to someone in school, or were mean to a sibling. For what do they need to be forgiven? Make sure to remind them that we are all human, and sometimes we do not act as lovingly as we should, but that God's forgiveness is always there, and there will always be more invitations to be generous, kind and loving to our families, friends, and even strangers!

Allow time for reflection. Distribute pencils and ask students to write their response on the back of the play money. Once the prayers are written, invite the listeners to approach the prayer table, one at a time, and to ignite the paper money to the candle and drop it into the coffee can to burn. This symbolic gesture will illustrate the need to let go of sin and to trust in God's forgiving love.

Conclusion

In conclusion, join hands and pray The Lord's Prayer.

31 Prayer Guide

Goal
To create a prayer guide to use every day for a month.

Gather
- Copy machine
- Paper
- Pencils or pens

Guide
"Thirty days has September, April, June, and November, when short February's done, all the rest have 31!" This familiar children's rhyme provides an easy way to remember the number of days in each month of the year. Creating a 31 (or 28, 29, or 30) day prayer guide offers an easy way to remember others in prayer every day for a month.

Prepare a prayer guide in the form of a calendar that can be used by members of the class, and the congregation, every day for a month. Ideas for prayer concerns include the names of the people in the class, the names of people who work in the parish, families in the congregation, meetings taking place during the month, countries where needs are great, and organizations that provide help for others. Information on specific events that will take place during the month, such as a meeting of the catechists, a food drive, or a birthday, could be incorporated into prayer petitions for specific days.

Explain the purpose of the project to the class and determine the theme of the calendar. Work together to compile a list of prayer concerns for every day of the month. Assemble the requests into a prayer guide—handwritten or typed—that can be duplicated and distributed to each student and to the entire congregation, if desired. Challenge the participants to remember the people and projects listed on the prayer guide every day of the month.

▶

Examples of prayer petitions related to HIV and AIDS concerns for a 31 day month include:

Pray for people who will be tested for HIV infection today.

Remember medical workers who provide care for persons with AIDS.

Say a prayer that persons addicted to drugs may find ways to address this problem.

Pray for the meeting of the AIDS Ministry committee that will be held today.

Pray for persons who will view the exhibit of the NAMES Project AIDS Memorial Quilt today.

Pray for care partners.

Pray for persons who share long kept secrets related to their sexual orientation.

Pray for parents who are grieving the loss of a child.

Pray for teachers who educate children about AIDS related themes.

Pray for denominational executives who make AIDS related statements.

Pray for school board members who make AIDS related policy decisions.

Pray for persons who live with guilt for transmitting the virus to someone else.

Pray for persons who counsel people with HIV/AIDS.

Pray for children who must decide whether or not to play with someone with HIV or AIDS.

Pray for scientists who seek to find a cure for the virus.

Pray for children who have lost parents to AIDS.

Pray for people who have become infected through blood transfusions.

Pray for medical supplies for countries in need.

Pray for volunteers for AIDS ministry organizations.

Pray for funding for AIDS related projects and programs.

Pray for the President of the United States and for the Congress who make AIDS related decisions.

Pray for legislators to pass laws that are fair to all people.

Pray for the interfaith worship service for the healing of AIDS that will be held today.

Pray that people who need medical treatment will find access to complete and compassionate care.

Pray that people will view sexuality as a gift from God.

Pray that persons with AIDS will find comfort from the Scriptures and from caring individuals and congregations.

Pray for volunteers to meet the numerous needs related to HIV and AIDS.

Pray for persons who are facing the loss of control of their bodies and their lives due to weakness and dementia.

Pray for conflict resolution in families facing AIDS related illness.

Pray for husbands and wives who have been infected by a spouse.

Pray for those who face the loss of their life at an early age.

㉜ Names of Jesus

Goal
To use a variety of names of Jesus as prayer salutations.

Gather
- Bibles
- Glue
- Magazines
- Markers
- Newspapers
- Newsprint
- Poster board
- Scissors

Guide
When the angel Gabriel appeared to Mary with the Good News that she would be the mother of the Savior, he also told her that the newborn's name was to be Jesus. In Hebrew, this name means "The Lord is salvation." Throughout history, there have been many names given to this child. Gain a better understanding of the person and work of Jesus by using a variety of names as prayer salutations.

A salutation is a form of greeting or address. Just as a letter begins with a salutation addressed to the person receiving the correspondence, a prayer generally starts with a salutation addressed to God, Jesus, or the Holy Spirit. Besides starting a prayer with the words "Dear Jesus," there are many ways to greet the second person of the Trinity. As individuals, small groups, or a class, brainstorm thirty-two ways to address Jesus at the beginning of a prayer. Although numerous names are possible, use the number 32 as a goal. Review the list of 32 names provided or compile a new one. Look through the Bible for suggestions.

▶

Suggested Names

Babe of Bethlehem
Bread of Life
Bright and Morning Star
Christ
Companion
Door
Emmanuel
Eternal Friend
Everlasting One
Forgiving One
Gentle One
Good Shepherd
Healer
King of Kings
Light of the World
Lord
Lord of Lords
Master
Messiah
Mighty God
Our Brother
Prince of Peace
Rabbi
Rose of Sharon
Salvation
Savior
Son of the Most High
Star of David
Teacher
Vine
Wonderful Counselor
Word

After the names have been reviewed or selected create a collage. Find pictures that depict the meaning of each name. For example, for Lord, use pictures of people and places throughout the world to symbolize that Jesus is Lord of all. Cut out the pictures, arrange the illustrations for each name as a group, and glue them to the poster board. Cut out letters to spell the name and glue it on top of or over the pictures. Fill the entire surface of the poster board to complete the collage.

Use a different name each time a prayer is offered or invite 32 different people to each address Jesus in a meaningful way.

33 Jesus' Passion

Goal

To create a round robin prayer thanking God for Jesus' life, death, and resurrection.

Gather

- Bibles
- Copy machine
- Paper
- Pencils or pens
- Resource sheet:
  - 11 x 3 = 33 Crossword Puzzle

Advance Preparation

- Make a copy of the resource sheet for each participant.

Guide

Most people think that Jesus was 33 at the time of his death. Since Jesus began his earthly ministry at the age of thirty, and it continued for three years (Luke 13:7), that would mean that Jesus was 33 at the time that he died, was buried, and arose from the grave, victorious over sin and death. For that reason, the number 33 is connected with this prayer lesson.

Begin by distributing a crossword puzzle sheet and a pencil or pen to each student. Challenge the group to answer 11 questions about Jesus' life, death, and resurrection. Note that all of the questions and answers focus on the number three: 11 x 3 = 33! Pass out Bibles so the participants may look up Scripture references if they have questions about the answers.

Once the crossword puzzles are solved review the answers.

Gather the participants and ask them to sit in a circle on the floor or on chairs. Invite the students to use the ideas in the questions and answers to create a round robin prayer thanking God for Jesus' life, death, and resurrection. Explain that Round Robin is a cooperative method of telling a story. In this lesson, it is used as a cooperative method of constructing a prayer. In a Round Robin, each participant adds a certain number of words to a sentence or statement. In this case, each person will have an opportunity, in turn, to add three words to a prayer. Begin the prayer for the group with three words, such as "Thank You, God...."

Go around the circle and provide an opportunity, as well as cues and encouragement, for each participant to contribute to the prayer. It might be helpful to structure the activity by introducing new themes such as Jesus' life, ministry, crucifixion, and resurrection. Continue until the prayer seems to be concluded or until the students run out of ideas. End the prayer with a summarizing sentence such as "We love you," or the word "Amen."

Challenge the group to continue to thank God for Jesus' life, death, and resurrection in three ways everyday—through their thoughts, words, and actions.

11 x 3 = 33 Crossword Puzzle

Clues

1. Peter, James, and John were the three _____ in the Garden of Gethsemane with Jesus. (Matthew 26:36-46)

2. God, Jesus, and the Holy Spirit are called the _____.

3. Peter _____ Jesus three times. (Matthew 26:69-75)

4. Jesus _____ on the third day. (Matthew 28:1-7)

5. Jesus was tempted by _____ three times. (Matthew 4:1-11)

6. There were three _____ at Calvary. (Matthew 27:38)

7. Jesus, Mary, and Joseph are called the Holy _____.

8. The veil of the _____ was torn in two at three o'clock, the third hour. (Matthew 27:45-54)

9. After the resurrection, Jesus asked _____ three times, "Do you love me?" (John 21:15-19)

10. Jesus was in the _____ for three days. (Matthew 27:62-65)

11. The message of Jesus' ministry is summed up in the word _____. (John 3:16)

Answers: 1. Disciples 2. Trinity 3. Denied 4. Arose 5. Satan 6. Crosses 7. Family 8. Temple 9. Peter 10. Tomb 11. Love

PRAYING BY NUMBER

34 Body Postures

Goal

To understand that the body is the temple of the Holy Spirit and to introduce a variety of body postures for prayer.

Gather

- Bible
- Equipment to play music
- Markers
- Newsprint
- Recording of "Hand in Hand" by Joe Wise
- Recording of tranquil background music

Guide

The human body is a marvelous gift from God. Take a few minutes to think of many of the wonderful things that the human body can do. Invite the participants to share responses and try to record 34 of them on newsprint. For example, the human body can crawl, jump, kneel, run, sit, stand, and walk. It can eat, hear, listen, see, sleep, smell, talk, and wake-up. The body can dance, fight, hug, kiss, learn, love, recite, remember, study, touch, and work. It can walk arm in arm, shake hands, pray, hold a baby, feel God's presence, embrace, cradle a puppy, and clasp a hand. Remind the listeners that since the human body is a gift from God, body movements can—and should—be used to offer praise and thanks to God through prayer.

Ask for examples of ways in which body postures are used during prayer. Answers may include closing eyes, folding hands, and kneeling. Organize the students into small groups and distribute newsprint and markers to each team. Encourage the learners to generate a list of various body postures used in prayer. For example:

1. *Eyes open*
2. *Eyes closed*
3. *Head raised*
4. *Head bowed*
5. *Kneeling*
6. *Standing*
7. *Sitting*
8. *Hands folded*
9. *Hands raised over head*
10. *Hands in "praying hands" position*
11. *Hands resting in lap*
12. *Hands holding rosary*
13. *Hands extended in front of body with palms up*

14. *Holding hands*
15. *Linking arms*
16. *Genuflecting*
17. *Lying on back*
18. *Lying face down*
19. *Bowing*
20. *Walking*
21. *Processing*
22. *Shoulder to shoulder in a crowd*
23. *Sitting cross legged*
24. *Arms folded across chest*
25. *Hand held over heart*
26. *Eyes looking into someone's eyes*
27. *Eyes fixed on object*
28. *Feet tapping*
29. *Lips moving*
30. *Speaking*
31. *Thinking*
32. *Embracing*
33. *Laying on of hands*
34. *Sign of the cross*

Once the small groups have completed the task, reconvene the class and compile one list containing at least 34 body postures for prayer. Remind the participants that Scripture tells us to use our bodies to glorify God. In fact, the Bible says that the body is the temple of the Holy Spirit.

Gather the group in a circle on chairs or on the floor and conclude the lesson with a brief prayer service.

To create a mood for prayer, lower the lights in the room and play tranquil background music. Encourage the participants to sit comfortably and to become silent and peaceful.

Prayer Service

Scripture Reading: 1 Corinthians 6:19-20

Do you not know that your body is a temple of the Holy Spirit within you, which you have from God, and that you are not your own? For you were bought with a price; therefore glorify God in your body.

Ritual Action

God our Creator, free my perception to see your image in myself.

Close your eyes. Sit comfortably in your chair, feet on the floor, hands in your lap. Tune into your breathing, in and out, breathing in the very breath of God, the Spirit of Life. Be aware of your body. Control the tension. Relax your feet. Wiggle your toes and ankles. Flex and relax the muscles in your legs. Flex and relax your abdominal muscles. Flex and relax the systems in the lower half of your body.

Expand your chest, inhale, and exhale deeply. Open and close your mouth widely. Flex and relax your face muscles, exercising the jaw. Turn your head from side to side, up and down, relax your muscles. Rotate and roll your shoulder muscles and relax them. Flex and relax your arm muscles, raising them high and lowering them. Become aware of your hands and fingers. Now, without opening your eyes extend your hands on either side and find two other hands to hold. Pray silently for the people whose hands you are holding. Ask God to be near to these people. Thank God for the wonderful gift of the body. When you are ready, open your eyes.

Closing Song

"Hand in Hand"

As the students leave, challenge them to experiment with a variety of postures for prayer in the next few days.

35 Creation

Goal

To write musical prayers thanking God for the gift of creation.

Gather

- Bible
- Markers
- Newsprint
- Tape, masking

Advance Preparation

Prepare a sheet of newsprint for each of these headings:

- Seven Days of Creation
- Seven Days of the Week
- Seven Continents
- Seven of the Planets
- Seven Note Names of a Musical Scale

Hang the newsprint sheets in the room.

Guide

In Hebrew, the primary root of the word seven means "to be complete." Creation offers the perfect example of seven as a number of completeness. In Genesis 2:1-3 the Bible tells us, "Thus the heavens and the earth were finished, and all their multitude. And on the seventh day God finished the work that he had done, and he rested on the seventh day from all the work that he had done. So God blessed the seventh day and hallowed it, because on it God rested from all the work that he had done in creation."

Since there are several sevens associated with creation and since there are also seven names for the eight notes on a musical scale, this prayer lesson will combine these two themes. Five sets of sevens—or 35—is the catalyst for composing musical prayers and thanking God for the gift of creation.

Direct the student's attention to the five sheets of newsprint that are hanging in the room.

Challenge the students to work together to list the correct set of seven on each sheet. Organize the class into five teams and provide markers for each group. Allow seven minutes for the activity. Provide hints and help as needed. At the end of seven minutes, call time and review the answers.

▸

49

Seven Days of Creation
1. Light
2. Firmament
3. Earth/Sea
4. Sun/Moon/Stars
5. Fish/Fowl
6. Animals/Humans
7. Rest

Seven Days of the Week
1. Sunday
2. Monday
3. Tuesday
4. Wednesday
5. Thursday
6. Friday
7. Saturday

Seven Continents
1. Africa
2. Antarctica
3. Asia
4. Australia
5. Europe
6. North America
7. South America

Seven (of the Eight) Planets
1. Earth
2. Jupiter
3. Mars
4. Mercury
5. Neptune
6. Saturn
7. Uranus
8. Venus

Seven Note Names of a Musical Scale
1. Do - C
2. Re - D
3. Me - E
4. Fa - F
5. So - G
6. La - A
7. Ti - B

Invite the group to write musical prayers to thank God for the gift of creation. Instruct the students to remain in the five groups and provide newsprint and markers for each team. Challenge each group to use the tune "Row, Row, Row Your Boat" to write a prayer on the theme of creation.

Sing the song "Row, Row, Row Your Boat" one or two times to review the tune and then show the students new words to it, such as:

> Thank you, God, for day and night,
> for sun and stars and moon.
> For flowers and trees and birds and bees
> we raise our prayerful tune!
> Every day of the week
> is a gift from you.
> We pray that we may honor God
> in everything we do.

Allow time for the groups to compose their musical prayers. When the assignment is completed, ask each group to share their song with the other students. Invite everyone to sing them together.

The messages may be extended by compiling songbooks and sharing them with other classes.

36 Growth Chart

Goal

To construct a 36 inch chart to record spiritual growth.

Gather

- Containers
- Glue
- Magazines, recycled
- Markers
- Paint brushes
- Paint, water color trays
- Paper, butcher or poster type – 36" long per person
- Pencils
- Scissors
- Water
- Yardsticks

Guide

Twelve inches in a foot—three feet in a yard—36 inches in a yardstick! A yardstick is a graduated measuring tool that's one yard in length. It is often used to measure a person's physical growth. In this prayer lesson, 36 inches will be used to help each believer measure spiritual growth, or maturity, in her or his relationship with God.

Ask if anyone has ever seen a growth chart. Commercial varieties come in assorted designs and are used as room decorations. Homemade versions include marks on doors or walls that record a young person's height from year to year. Doctor's offices usually have posters that measure physical development. In this prayer lesson, however, students will use a 36 inch yardstick to measure spiritual growth.

Tell the students that over the next few days, or weeks, each person will make a spiritual growth chart—a poster to measure their growing relationship with God. Prayer is an important part of growing in union with God. Everyone needs to ask God to help them live a life that measures up to God's standards. Everyone also needs to remember family and friends—and total strangers—in prayer. Examples of using prayer to mature spiritually include thanking God for food, repeating the Lord's Prayer, offering praise for the new day, and remembering a classmate who is sick.

Dispense the butcher or poster paper, pencils, and yardsticks to the participants. Instruct them to use a yardstick and pencil to measure and mark 36 one-inch sections on the left side of the paper. Tell the learners that they will record one special growth experience through prayer on each line. Each one-inch mark will measure a way in which they grew in their relationship with God. Allow time to make the yardstick posters, reminding students to add their names to the charts. When the growth charts are constructed, hang them in the room.

Once 36 prayer experiences are recorded, invite the learners to cut photos and words from old magazines and/or to paint watercolor pictures to illustrate their progress.

Once the project is completed, allow the students to take the posters home to share with others.

Remind the pupils that although physical growth may come to a standstill, spiritual and emotional growth is a life-long process. Challenge each person to continue to cultivate a relationship with God—especially through prayer—every day.

37 Symbols

Goal

To use 37 symbolic items to create a worship center as an environment for prayer.

Gather

- Copy machine
- Equipment to play music
- Objects to be used in creating sacred space for a prayer experience, such as:
  - Basin
  - Basket
  - Bible
  - Bookmark
  - Bottle or carafe of grape juice
  - Bottle or carafe of wine
  - Bread, loaf
  - Candle holders
  - Candles, two
  - Chalice
  - Cross
  - Fabric, liturgical color or seasonal theme
  - Flask for oil
  - Flowers, fresh
  - Grapes, three bunches – green, purple, red
  - Incense stick
  - Incense holder
  - Matches, two
  - Napkins, two
  - Oil
  - Pitcher
  - Plate for bread
  - Ribbon
  - Stand for Bible
  - Table
  - Table cloth
  - Towel
  - Vase
  - Water
  - Water for flowers
  - Wheat
- Paper
- Recording of "Prayer for Peace" by David Haas
- Resource sheet:
  - "Treasure Hunt Clue Cards"
- Table, 6'-8'

Advance Preparation

- Set a 6'- 8' table in the center of the room.
- Duplicate the resource sheets double-sided and cut the cards apart.
- Distribute the items throughout the room.

Guide

Although prayer can be offered to God in any place, a worship center—or sacred space—fosters a spirit of reverence. In this prayer lesson 37 symbolic items are used to create an environment for prayer.

As the participants arrive, invite them to form a circle around the empty table. Ask the students to name some of the uses for a table. Responses might include eating a family meal, doing homework, writing a letter, and playing a game. Tell the group that a table can also be used as a worship center—a special place for prayer.

Invite the students to participate in a treasure hunt to find objects for creating the sacred space. Organize learners into 12 teams. Depending on the number of students, a team may be one person! Distribute a clue card to each team, warn participants not to look at the reverse side until it is time, and review the procedure. Assure all the groups that help will be offered as needed.

After the leader reads the first clue, Team One will get up quietly, look around the room, and find the item(s) that fit the description. The group will place them on the prayer table, then turn over the card and perform any additional action as described. One person or the entire team may read the prayer out loud. Then the group members will quietly return to their seats. Continue until all clues have been read, and then proceed with a time of prayer and reflection.

Once all of the prayer objects have been placed in the worship space, ignite the candle and incense stick, pour water into the basin and grape juice or wine into the cup, and conclude with the following prayer service.

▸

Symbols Prayer Service

Opening Prayer

Leader: Your Word, O God, is power, hope, and truth.

All: We have seen it with our own eyes and stand in awe and wonder.

Leader: You have chosen the small and the weak to lift up the strong.

All: And have called the foolish to confound the wise.

Leader: We have seen Your glory made holy and real in the little ones of the earth.

All: And radiant in the eyes of the vulnerable.

Leader: You take the ordinary

All: and transform it into the extraordinary.

Leader: You take the common

All: and create the sacred.

Song

"Prayer for Peace" by David Haas

Reading

So, Jesus began to form his group of disciples. Apart from Peter and Andrew and James and John, there were Philip and Bartholomew, who also came from Galilee. Then there was Matthew, who used to be a tax collector, and Simon the Zealot who used to be (and probably still was) a rebel! After them came Thomas, a twin, Jude, Judas, and another James.

As they travelled from village to village and from town to town, they learned all they could from Jesus. They heard his stories many times and watched the way he dealt with people. They all agreed, he was the most remarkable man they had ever met.

One day, they had stopped by a well for lunch and were talking as usual.

"Well," said Simon, sitting back with a satisfied sigh, "When do we start?" "When do we start what?" said Jesus. "He means when do we start the revolution," said Judas Iscariot, polishing the blade of his dagger, "When do we proclaim you as king and gather together an army?"

Jesus raised his hand for silence. "I keep trying to explain that I'm not that sort of king. I haven't come to put people to death; I've come to offer them life! You ask, 'when do you begin?' My answer is, we have begun. This is it! Sharing our life, trusting God, and letting tomorrow take care of itself. Look at the flowers—do they worry about what to wear? And the birds—doesn't God look after them? So why are you fussing? Let's be glad that we belong to God and leave our problems to God."

Leader Reflection

Jesus came to bring peace and love, not war and hatred. As a sign of our belief in Jesus, I invite each of you, one at a time, to come to the prayer table and touch your hand to the refreshing water. Give thanks to God for the ordinary that is extraordinary, for the common that is sacred. Then, break off a piece of bread and eat it, remembering Jesus words, "Do this in memory of me." When you are finished, reverently return to your seat.

Song

"Prayer for Peace"

Conclusion

At the conclusion of the prayer service, challenge the group to look for the extraordinary in the ordinary and the sacred in the common.

Treasure Hunt Clue Cards 1/8

CLUE 1

Clothing for a table

CLUE 2

Dispels darkness;
Symbol of Jesus as the Light

CLUE 3

The Word of God

Treasure Hunt Clue Cards 2/8

Item 1
Table cloth and seasonal fabric

Action
Cover table with cloth and place seasonal fabric in the center.

Prayer
Loving and good God,
as the grass of the field
is clothed in your beauty,
so too are we clothed
in your grace and wonder.

Like this table dressed in beauty,
may we stand before you
longing to praise and worship you
above all else. Amen.

Item 2
Candles, candle holders, and matches

Action
Place candles in holders and set on table. Lay matches near candles.

Prayer
God of all creation,
giver of your Son Jesus
as the Light to the nations,
give us the ability
to glow in Christian love
and care as Jesus did
in the midst of darkness and hurt.

Give us the capacity to ever live
in the light of Christ.

Amen

Item 3
Bible, stand for Bible, and bookmark

Action
Set Bible on stand and place bookmark in Bible.

Prayer
In the beginning was the Word,
and the Word was with God,
and the Word was God.

Loving God, through the power of your word humanity was ever changed.

Jesus your only Son walked with us, lived with us, dreamed our dreams, and gave us New Life.

Help us to humbly hear the Word, take it to heart, and put it into action. Amen.

Treasure Hunt Clue Cards 3/8

CLUE 4

Holy smoke

CLUE 5

A fresh cut garden

CLUE 6

Used for anointing

Treasure Hunt Clue Cards 4/8

Item 4

Incense stick, holder, and matches

Action

Insert incense stick into holder and place on table. Set matches nearby.

Prayer

Let my prayer rise like incense before you, my God.

Heavenly God, hearer of all prayers, listen to us now as we raise our hopes and dreams before you like burning incense.

We know that you hear our every word; give us the courage to respond to yours.

Amen.

Item 5

Table cloth and seasonal fabric

Action

Vase of fresh flowers in water.

Prayer

God, giver of life and beauty, before us in this vase of flowers we see your lovely creation.

We ask you to guide us as we try to walk gently among your living world and to be the best stewards of the earth we can be.

Amen.

Item 6

Flash of sweet smelling oil

Action

Place flask of oil on table.

Prayer

God, anoint us with the oil of your salvation.

Give us the ability to look and act as your redeemed children so that, in building the Kingdom here on earth, we may bring more people to you and your Son Jesus, who is Lord forever.

Amen.

PRAYING BY NUMBER

Treasure Hunt Clue Cards 5/8

CLUE 7

Then Jesus proceeded
to wash their feet.

CLUE 8

Fruit of the vine

CLUE 9

A drink made from
the fruit of the vine

Treasure Hunt Clue Cards 6/8

Item 7
Pitcher of water, basin, and towel

Action
Place pitcher of water in basin and drape towel over it.

Prayer
Dear God, your Son Jesus by his great example showed us the true way of service. He took water and washed the feet of his friends. This great act of love and care illustrated the humility of Jesus' compassion. Teach us true love and compassion in the service we show to others in our day to day living. Give us the keen insight that Jesus had to reach out with a cup of water to those who are thirsty. Amen.

Item 8
Three bunches of grapes—green, purple, and red, napkin, and basket

Action
Spread the napkin in the basket and place the grapes in it.

Prayer
Again, Lord, we are reminded of the wonder of your created earth.

The lush beauty of the grapes placed on this table fill us with the anticipation of your sweetness.

We thank you for all the gifts you have bestowed upon us; especially for the gift of your Son, who is our Lord and Savior.

Amen.

Item 9
Bottle of grape juice, bottle of wine, and chalice

Action
Place the grape juice, wine, and chalice on the table.

Prayer
During the wedding feast at Cana Jesus turned water into wine, thus performing the first sign of his glory, and his disciples believed in him.

God, help us to believe in the power of Jesus' life and in all that he stood for.

Help change us, especially in our times of unbelief and doubt. We ask this in the name of Jesus, the one who changed the face of the earth. Amen.

PRAYING BY NUMBER

Treasure Hunt Clue Cards 7/8

CLUE 10

A grain of the field

CLUE 11

Food made from wheat

CLUE 12

Symbol of salvation

PRAYING BY NUMBER

Treasure Hunt Clue Cards 8/8

Item 10

Wheat and ribbon

Action

Place the wheat on the table and tie ribbon around it.

Prayer

A grain of wheat must fall to the ground and die before it can bear fruit.

God of heaven and earth,
fill us with the seeds of new life,
so all that we do in your honor and name will blossom and be fruitful.

Help us to die to greed, hate, and selfishness, so that the fruit of peace will reign in our world.
We ask this in Jesus' name. Amen.

Item 11

Loaf of bread, napkin, bread basket or plate

Action

Spread napkin in basket and place loaf of bread in it.

Prayer

Holy One, help us to remember that when we gather to share bread, it is done to honor Jesus. We recall at the Last Supper, how Jesus took bread, blessed it, broke it, and gave it to his disciples (and now to us) saying eat this and whenever you do remember me and my endless love for you. We ask, Almighty God, that you feed our mind, heart, and soul with the food of Jesus, that we may always walk the path of holiness. Amen.

Item 12

Cross

Action

Place the cross in the worship center.

Prayer

God of Salvation,
thank you for the gift of your Son, Jesus, our Savior.

Amen.

PRAYING BY NUMBER

38 Spontaneous Prayer

Goal

To create a scrapbook to record everyday experiences as moments of prayer.

Gather

- Glue sticks
- Hole punch
- Magazines, recycled
- Markers
- Paper, colored and white construction – two pieces per person
- Pencils
- Resource sheet:
  - "Finding God in Everyday Life"
- Ribbon, twine, or yarn
- Scissors

Guide

Life is full of graceful moments of prayer. Consider thanking God for food while washing dishes, recognizing God's gift of an able mind while entering data into a computer, and praising God for the dependability of creation as morning follows night—day after day. Prayer offers an opportunity to bring God into every moment of every day. Spontaneous prayer offers the opportunity to pray about anything, anywhere, anytime. This lesson provides a way to recognize and to remember these prayerful moments through the construction of a prayer scrapbook.

Ask the students to name times during the day when they pray. Answers may include at mealtime, before a test, and at bedtime. Ask the group if anyone has ever prayed while looking at a flower, holding a baby, or building a sandcastle. Prayer can—and should—be offered to God in adoration, confession, thanksgiving, and supplication at any time of any day. This type of spontaneous—spur-of-the-moment—silent or spoken prayer helps us recognize God in every part of life.

Explain that the learners will have the opportunity to make prayer scrapbooks. Ask a volunteer to define the word "scrapbook." Note that a scrapbook is a book that people make to help them remember special times in life. For example, a ticket stub from a play or concert, a paper napkin from a birthday party, or a card or letter from a loved one might be glued to a page of a scrapbook to remind the person of the special time. A prayer scrapbook will provide a way to record the opportunities for spontaneous prayer that occur every day.

▶

Distribute two pieces of white construction paper and five or six sheets of colored paper to each learner. Instruct them to make a book by placing the colored paper between the two pieces of white paper. Hole punch and tie the pages together with ribbon, twine, or yarn. Using markers, direct the students to letter the phrase "_____ Prayer Scrapbook" on the front cover, printing their own name in the blank. Invite the participants to design a cover.

Tell the learners that their scrapbooks will be used to record special moments for prayer that occur every day. Any number of prayer moments can be used for the activity, but 38 could be a goal or a guide. The list of 38 experiences on the resource sheet might serve as an inventory of graceful prayer moments or the students may compile their own list.

The prayer scrapbooks may be completed in several ways. To do the project in class, provide old magazines, scissors, glue, and markers. Direct the group to print "Prayer Moment" headings on the pages of the scrapbook. Several can be written on the same page. Next, they should find pictures and words in the magazines, cut them out, and glue them in the appropriate places to depict their prayer moments. Illustrations may be drawn with markers, too.

To finish the project at home, direct the pupils to take the scrapbooks with them and to complete the pages as prayer moments occur or at the end of each day. These moments may be portrayed with magazine pictures, drawings, or actual objects. At a specified time, ask the students to bring the books to class to share their experiences with others. Encourage the learners to use the scrapbooks to remind them of the spontaneous opportunities for prayer every day.

As an alternative to a paper scrapbook, use a digital format to create the project.

Finding God in Everyday Life

An Inventory of Graceful Moments

Prayer moments, followed by ideas for what items can be placed in a scrapbook to remember them.

1. A walk in the woods
   Leaf, twig, acorn

2. Baked bread or a cake
   Flour, eggs

3. Felt the rain
   Drops of water, poem, picture of rain storm

4. Made a snow person
   Photos of winter

5. Walked hand in hand
   Pictures of friends

6. A family meal
   Food, dinner napkin

7. Holding a baby
   Pictures of infants, baby animals

8. Went to a wedding or anniversary party
   A love letter

9. A night walk
   Paper stars

10. Heard beautiful music
    Music notes

11. Cared for someone who was sick
    Band aid

12. Went to a ballet
    Program, poem

13. Opening a special present
    Ribbon, wrapping paper

14. You cried
    Paper tissue

15. You laughed
    Cartoon strip

16. You were hugged
    Pictures of arms

17. Someone close to you died
    Photo, prayer

18. You were ill
    Get well card

19. A special Christmas
    Photo, candy cane

20. A special birthday
    Candles, card, the year

21. You took a big risk
    Letter to yourself

22. You failed at something
    Prayer, poem

23. You were captured by the beauty of nature
    Photo, picture, paper sun

24. A walk in a snow storm
    Paper snow flakes

25. Working in the garden
    Dirt, seeds

26. A special Easter
    Easter lily, cross

27. Time with a special friend
    Prayer of thanks

28. You felt guilty
    Prayer of forgiveness

29. Someone forgave you
    Any memory of the event

30. You forgave someone else
    Note of forgiveness

31. You thought about death
    Psalm 23

32. You walked the dog
    Dog

33. You played on the beach
    Sand, sea shells

34. You laid on the grass with your face to the sun
    Blades of grass, splashes of yellow paint

35. Visited someone who was homebound
    Write a memory that was shared

36. You drank hot chocolate
    Marshmallow

37. Ate your favorite fruit
    Fruit

38. Loved yourself
    Another love letter

PRAYING BY NUMBER

🏉 Prayer Chain

Goal

To make a prayer chain illustrating the Heart of Jesus' Love to use to encircle a prayer space or a prayer table

Gather

- Candle, red
- Cloth for prayer table, white
- Copy machine
- Equipment to play music
- Glue sticks
- Matches
- Paper, construction – red and various colors
- Paper, white
- Pencils
- Pens
- Recording of tranquil music
- Resource sheets:
  - "Heart of Jesus' Love"
  - "Heart Patterns"
- Rulers
- Scissors
- Table

Advance Preparation

- Dress the prayer table with the white cloth and red candle.
- Duplicate the resource sheets.

Guide

Hold up a red paper heart. Ask the participants what they think of when they see the red shape. Allow students to share ideas, for example: Valentine's Day, love, friendship, Mom and Dad, a human organ. Ask if the heart reminds them of Jesus. If students answer yes, ask why they gave that response. The heart of Jesus is full of love for all people. Let the listeners share their responses.

Tell the group that they will be creating hearts to use in a special prayer service.

Distribute red construction paper, pencils, pens, heart patterns, and scissors. Instruct the participants to trace and cut 39 red hearts. Tell them that the hearts will be combined to create a prayer chain to be used in the prayer service. Once the hearts have been completed, dispense the "Heart of Jesus' Love" resource sheets. Invite the learners to copy the words onto separate hearts.

Next, direct the students to cut 39 strips of construction paper to be used in making a paper chain. The strips should be one inch by eight inches. Once the strips are cut, tell the group to use a glue stick and to attach a red heart to the center of each strip. Now, direct the participants to use glue to link the heart/strips together to form a paper chain. Once the chain has been completed, carefully move it to the area prepared for the prayer service. Use the linked hearts to encircle the worship space or prayer table. Gather the students on the floor or on chairs and conclude the activity by using the following prayer service.

▸

Prayer Service

Begin by igniting the candle and playing tranquil music.

Opening Prayer

Leader:

O Christ our Lord,
perfect love for all humankind,
grant we ask of you
that love, wisdom, and understanding
ever live within us.

May we see deeper and deeper
the lesson of your holiness,
which is always before us.

Show us the heart of your love
so that we may show others
love and charity.

Gospel Reading

John 15:9-12

"As the Father has loved me, so I have loved you; abide in my love. If you keep my commandments, you will abide in my love, just as I have kept my Father's commandments and abide in his love. I have said these things to you so that my joy may be in you, and that your joy may be complete."

"This is my commandment, that you love one another as I have loved you."

Gospel Response

Using the prayer chain, invite students to read aloud the "Heart of Jesus' Love" statements. After each invocation, invite everyone to respond with the words, "Show us your love and mercy."

Dismissal

End the prayer service with The Lord's Prayer and an invitation to show one another a sign of Jesus' love—a hug, hand shake, or a group embrace.

Heart of Jesus' Love

1. Heart of Jesus, Son of the eternal Father
2. Heart of Jesus, formed by the Holy Spirit in Mary's womb
3. Heart of Jesus, united to the Word of God
4. Heart of Jesus, infinite in majesty
5. Heart of Jesus, God's holy temple
6. Heart of Jesus, house of the Most High
7. Heart of Jesus, house of God
8. Heart of Jesus, gate of heaven
9. Heart of Jesus, glowing furnace of charity
10. Heart of Jesus, vessel of love
11. Heart of Jesus, vessel of justice
12. Heart of Jesus, full of loving kindness
13. Heart of Jesus, deep well of all virtues
14. Heart of Jesus, worthy of all praise
15. Heart of Jesus, royal home of all hearts
16. Heart of Jesus, treasure-house of wisdom
17. Heart of Jesus, where abides the fullness of God
18. Heart of Jesus, in which God is well pleased
19. Heart of Jesus, of whose fullness we have all received
20. Heart of Jesus, desire of the eternal hills
21. Heart of Jesus, patient and kind
22. Heart of Jesus, rich in mercy
23. Heart of Jesus, bountiful to all who call upon you
24. Heart of Jesus, fount of life
25. Heart of Jesus, overwhelmed in sorrow
26. Heart of Jesus, bruised for our sin
27. Heart of Jesus, patient even unto the cross
28. Heart of Jesus, fountain of all consolation
29. Heart of Jesus, fount of holiness
30. Heart of Jesus, our life and resurrection
31. Heart of Jesus, our peace
32. Heart of Jesus, our atonement
33. Heart of Jesus, victim of all our sin
34. Heart of Jesus, happiness to them that trust in you
35. Heart of Jesus, hope of them that live for you
36. Heart of Jesus, delight of all hearts
37. Heart of Jesus, source of love and healing
38. Heart of Jesus, burns with the goodness of God
39. Heart of Jesus, vessel of love for all people

Heart Patterns

④⓿ Wilderness Experiences

Goal

To meditate on Jesus' 40-day wilderness experience and to illustrate this theme through a sand painting activity.

Gather

- Bibles, one per person
- Containers, one per color of sand
- Jars, small
- Paint, powered tempera in variety of colors
- Resource sheet
  - "List of Bible Passages"
- Sand, fine white
- Spoons
- Toothpicks, long and sturdy

Advance Preparation

- Put one cup of sand in each container. Add a different color of powdered tempera paint to each batch and stir until the sand is colored.
- Duplicate the resource sheet.

Guide

Forty, a number frequently found in Scripture, is a number that is often associated with testing and trial. In this prayer lesson 40 relates to the number of days Jesus spent in the wilderness during the period of his temptation by Satan.

Distribute a Bible to each participant or small group. Invite the students to look up several Old Testament and New Testament passages and to determine the number listed in each of them. The verses are:

- Genesis 7:4
- Exodus 3
- Exodus 24:18
- Numbers 13:25
- Numbers 14:33
- Deuteronomy 8:2
- 1 Samuel 17:16
- 1 Kings 19:8
- Jonah 3:4
- Matthew 4:2
- Mark 1:13
- Luke 4:2
- Acts 1:3

Ask the class to name the number mentioned in each of the Bible verses. The answer is 40. Tell the group that in this prayer lesson they will focus on the 40 days Jesus spent in the wilderness in deep communion with God, his Father, while he was tempted by Satan. Note that this story is found in Matthew 4:1-11, Mark 1:12, 13, and Luke 4:1-13. Read one of the Scripture accounts out loud.

▶

Provide an opportunity for the participants to experience wilderness quiet through Scripture meditation. Explain that meditation is a process of pondering or thinking. It relies on observation, fact finding, questioning, reflecting, analyzing, and understanding. Prayerful meditation is one way to think about the things of God. It is a combination of prayer, thoughts, and openness to God's guidance. In meditation, God is addressed and some deeper truth is considered while in God's presence. One of the best ways to meditate is to focus on a passage from the Bible. The New Testament passages Matthew 4:1-11, Mark 1:12, 13, and Luke 4:1-13—about Jesus' 40 days in the wilderness—provide the theme and direction for this prayer experience.

Explain that meditative prayer has three steps. The first step is to pray to the Holy Spirit asking for guidance as the passage is read. For example: "Dear God, send the Holy Spirit to help enlighten my mind to understand what it is you wish to show me during this time of meditation and through this Scripture passage. Draw my heart ever closer to you so my mind may stay focused on your Word. Help me to do whatever is necessary to fulfill your will for my life."

The second step is to sit comfortably and relax any tension in the body. Read the passage silently—slowly, carefully, and prayerfully. Try picturing the scene mentally. Ask the questions: Who is involved? What are they doing? Why? How? What is the point?

The third step is to pray that God will help you understand and live out the message of the Scripture passage.

Provide a Bible for each person and direct them to locate the wilderness passage in the Gospels. Allow time for the group to reflect on Jesus' forty-day experience.

Once all have had an opportunity to spend time with the Scripture passage ask the group to reflect on questions such as:

> What new meaning did you find in the passage?
> How does the passage relate to your life?
> What did the passage tell you about yourself and God's will for you?
> How can you live out God's message?

As a beautiful way to illustrate this wilderness experience, invite the learners to create sand paintings. Distribute a small glass jar and a long toothpick to each person. Place the colored sand and spoons within sharing distance of the students. Tell the students to spoon the first layer of colored sand into the jar. Cover one-fourth of the bottom of the jar with this color and smooth the top of the layer. Next, carefully spoon a second color of sand on top of the first. Demonstrate how to slide a long toothpick down the side of the jar to create designs in the sand. More layers may be added in this manner.

Display the wonderful sand creations as a way of remembering the 40 days that Jesus spent in the wilderness and the participant's own wilderness meditation experience.

List of Bible Passages

Forty	**Wilderness**
Genesis 7:4	*Matthew 4:1-11*
Exodus 3	*Mark 1:12, 13*
Exodus 24:18	*Luke 4:1-13*
Numbers 13:25	
Numbers 14:33	
Deuteronomy 8:2	
1 Samuel 17:16	
1 Kings 19:8	
Jonah 3:4	
Matthew 4:2	
Mark 1:13	
Luke 4:2	
Acts 1:3	

Resources

Caprio, Betsy. *Experiments In Prayer.* Notre Dame, IN: Ave Maria Press, 1973.

Cronin, Gaynell Bordes. *Holy Days and Holidays: Prayer Celebrations with Children* (2 volumes). San Francisco: Harper & Row, 1985, 1988.

Jessie, Karen. *Praying with Children Grades 4-6.* Villa Maria, PA: The Center for Learning, 1986.

Jones, Timothy and Jill Zook-Jones. *Prayer - Discovering What Scripture Says.* Wheaton, IL: Harold Shaw Publishers, 1993.

Manternach, Janaan with Carl J. Pfeifer. *And the Children Pray.* Notre Dame, IN: Ave Maria Press, 1989.

Mathson, Patricia. *Pray & Play: 28 Prayer Services and Activities for Children In K through Sixth Grade.* Notre Dame, IN: Ave Maria Press, 1989.

Rezy, Carol. *Liturgies for Little Ones: 38 Celebrations for Grades One to Three.* Notre Dame, IN: Ave Maria Press, 1978.

Smith, Judy Gattis. *Teaching Children about Prayer.* Prescott, AZ: Educational Ministries, 1988.

About the Author

Phyllis Vos Wezeman

As a religious educator, Phyllis Wezeman has served as Director of Christian Nurture at a downtown congregation in South Bend, Indiana, Executive Director of the Parish Resource Center of Michiana, and Program Coordinator for ecumenical as well as interfaith organizations in Indiana and Michigan.

In academics, Phyllis has been Adjunct Faculty in the Education Department at Indiana University South Bend and in the Department of Theology at the University of Notre Dame. She is an "Honorary Professor" of the Saint Petersburg (Russia) State University of Pedagogical Art where she has taught methods courses for extended periods on several occasions. She has also been guest lecturer at the Shanghai Teachers College in China.

As founder of the not-for-profit Malawi Matters, Inc., she develops and directs HIV & AIDS Education programs with thousands of volunteers in nearly 200 villages in Malawi, Africa including "Creative Methods of HIV & AIDS Education," "Culture & HIV-AIDS," and "Equipping Women/Empowering Girls."

Author or co-author of over 1,950 articles and books, she has written for over 80 publishers.

Phyllis served as President of Active Learning Associates, Inc.; a consultant or board member to numerous local and national organizations such as the American Bible Society, Church World Service, LOGOS, and the Peace Child Foundation; leader of a six-week youth exchange program to Russia and the Ukraine; and Project Director for four Lilley Worship Renewal grants. She is the recipient of three "Distinguished Alumni Awards" and recipient of the Aggiornamento Award from the Catholic Library Association.

Wezeman holds undergraduate degrees in Business, Communications, and General Studies from various institutions and an MS in Education from Indiana University South Bend.

Phyllis and her husband Ken (who met when they were in second and third grade in elementary school) have three children and their spouses, Stephanie (Jeff), David, and Paul (Deha), five grandchildren, Quin, Ayle, Lief, Ashley, and Jacob, and two great-grandsons, Maddox and Troy.

MORE RESOURCES BY phyllis vos wezeman

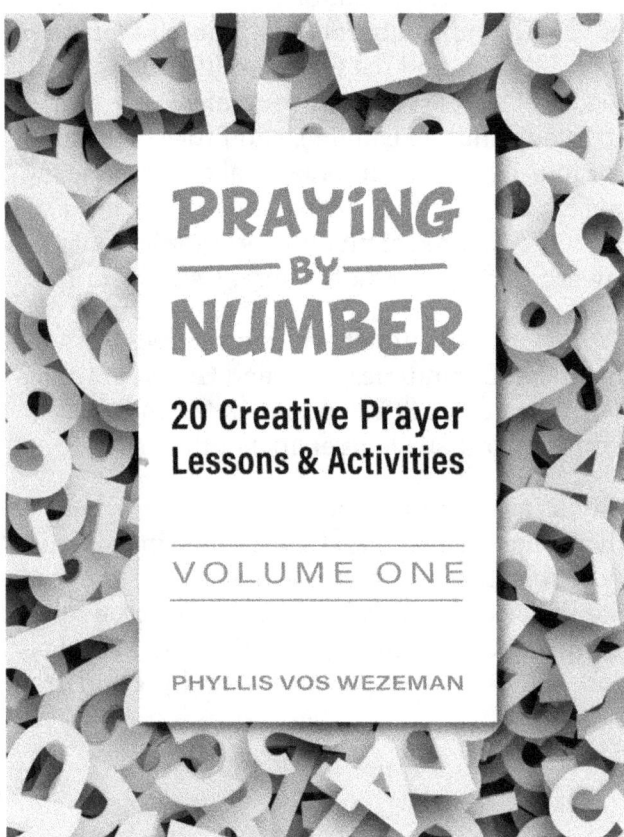

76 PAGES PER VOLUME • 8½"x11" • PW110

Praying by Number
Volume One
20 Creative Prayer Lessons & Activities

1. God
2. Prayer Partners
3. Trinity
4. Parts of Prayer
5. Senses
6. Jars of Water
7. Gifts of the Spirit
8. Beatitudes
9. Fruit of the Spirit
10. Commandments
11. The Lord's Prayer
12. The Apostles' Creed
13. Disciples
14. Works of Mercy
15. Stations of the Cross
16. Old Testament Prophets
17. Saint Patrick's Prayers
18. The Pharisee and the Publican
19. Gospels
20. Fingers and Toes

100 Creative Techniques for Teaching Bible Stories

In this treasure chest of fun ideas and activities, you'll find a wealth of practical possibilities for reviewing Scripture stories with the young and old. These easy-to-use techniques require very simple materials; for some you need only a Bible and your imagination. Each technique can be used for multiple purposes: to teach a prayer, to tell the story of a saint, or to enjoy a Scripture story in a new way. It is an ideal resource for catechists and religion teachers as well as for those preparing liturgies, summer programs, and intergenerational activities.

108 PAGES • 8½"x 11" • PW101

Experience the Saints

Activities for Multiple Intelligences

Eight activities per saint, each based on a different learning intelligence. Includes whole family and general classroom guides, with reproducible handouts.

- Vol. 1: Patrick, James, Hildegard of Bingen • PW201
- Vol. 2: Francis, Clare, Margaret of Scotland • PW202
- Vol. 3: Joan of Arc, Thomas Becket, Agnes • PW203
- Vol. 4: Peter, Catherine of Siena, Scholastica • PW204

200 PAGES PER VOLUME • 8½"x11"

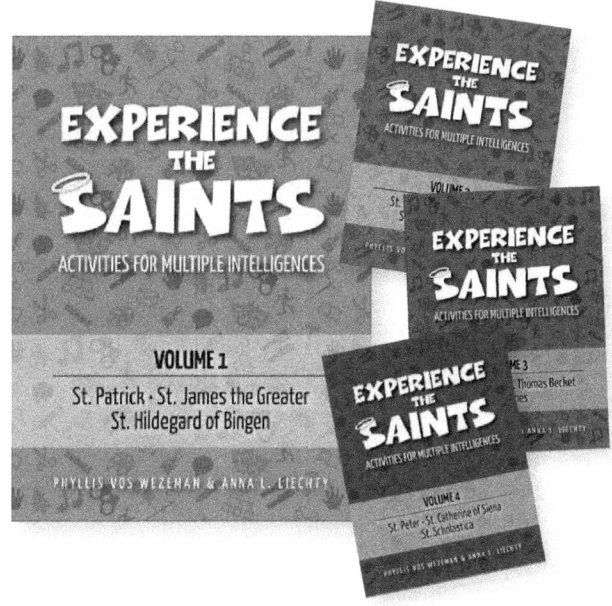

52 Interactive Bible Stories

A Collection of Action, Echo, Rhythm, and Syllable Stories

Participants will love these playful ways of expressing Scripture through a variety of storytelling techniques:. This delightful collection tells Bible stories in creative, interactive ways that will engage anyone from the toddlers through adulthood. They are a great way to add life to classes or retreat-like experiences. These playful stories involve the learner in the process and ensure that the Bible story is understood an internalized.

74 PAGES • 8½"x 11" • PW100

Seasons by Step: A Week-by-Week Thematic Approach

Use these creative approaches to explore a theme in-depth over the course of a season through Scripture. Each includes **talking points for children's messages, at-home family activities, artwork** for weekly symbols, and more.

Know Chocolate for Lent (Lent & Holy Week)

Uses the growing and manufacturing process of chocolate as a metaphor for the growth of faith and discipleship in the Christian life. Adult formation materials for a parish-wide approach are sold separately. • 80 PAGES • LR119

God's Family Tree (Lent & Holy Week)
Tracing the Story of Salvation

Tells the story of God's people as they struggle to find faith and hope for life through the symbols of trees found in Scripture. Includes optional Easter pageant and classroom activities. • 114 PAGES • LR116

In the Name of the Master (Advent/Christmas/Epiphany)
Sharing the Story of Christ

Uses a variation of the Advent wreath that uses fruits as symbols for the many names of God's Masterpiece, Jesus. Help your kids & families go deeper as they light their Advent candles each week. • 37 PAGES • LR108

• •

Joy to the World
International Christmas Crafts & Customs

Dozens of activities, from 12 countries that you can use again and again. Develop an appreciation for the contributions of the peoples of all lands and races to the celebration of Christmas. • 159 PAGES • 8½"x11" • LR104

Ideas A-Z
Crafts & Activities for Advent, Christmas, & Epiphany

Offers different theme or learning approach for each letter of the alphabet. Great ideas for intergenerational activities, lesson plans, or worship experiences. • 94 PAGES • 8½"x11" • PW102

Finding Your Way after Your Child Dies

Offers parents a comforting way to grieve. Easily adapted for use in small and large group settings such as a support group, prayer service, or family ministry session. 192 PAGES • IC937005

http://pastoral.center/phyllis-vos-wezeman

 The Pastoral Center *Pastoral ministers serving pastoral ministers*

http://pastoral.center • resources@pastoralcenter.com • Call us at 844-727-8672 (M-F 9am-5pm CT)

www.ingramcontent.com/pod-product-compliance
Lightning Source LLC
Chambersburg PA
CBHW080407170426
43193CB00016B/2841